Little Children's Bible Books

MOSES

Retold by Anne de Graaf

Illustrated by José Pérez Montero

BROADMAN
&HOLMAN
PUBLISHERS

MOSES

Published in 1999 by Broadman & Holman Publishers,
Nashville, Tennessee

Text copyright © 1998 Anne de Graaf
Illustration copyright © 1998 José Pérez Montero
Design by Ben Alex
Conceived, designed and produced by Scandinavia Publishing House

Printed in Hong Kong
ISBN 0-8054-1900-4

*Dedicated to José Pérez Montero's
grandchildren and to Amanda Potter*

Pharaoh had ordered his Egyptian soldiers to kill Hebrew babies like Moses. So Moses' mother put him in a basket and sent him floating down a river.

But God kept Moses safe.
And when he woke up and
started crying, Pharaoh's
daughter heard the baby
and saved him, making
Moses her own son.

Moses grew up in Pharaoh's palace. The Egyptians hated Hebrews, who were God's people. One day, Moses saw an Egyptian hitting a Hebrew man. Moses killed the Egyptian and ran away.

11

Moses hid in the desert for many years. One day he saw a bush on fire, but the fire was not really burning the bush! How could that be? It was God, trying to get Moses to listen.

What do YOU do to get people to listen?

What did God want to say? That Moses should go back to Egypt and help save God's people from the Egyptians. Moses was afraid and said, "Not me, God."

God knew Moses could not speak well, but God said he would help him. All Moses had to do was just say, "Yes."

If I asked you to hop ten times on your bed, would you say, "Yes?"

17

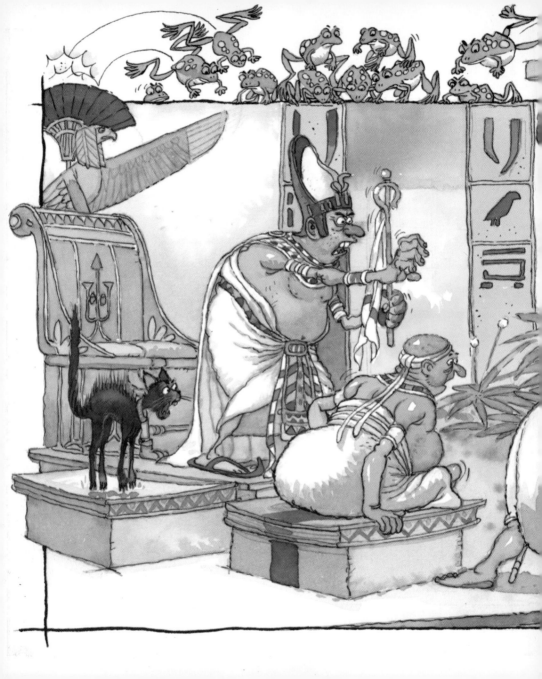

God made ten bad things happen to Egypt. These bad things were plagues, like turning the water red, and sending many frogs and insects.

Moses said, "Trust God!" And what did God do? He split the Red Sea right in half. Now every-one could cross through the middle of the water and still stay dry!

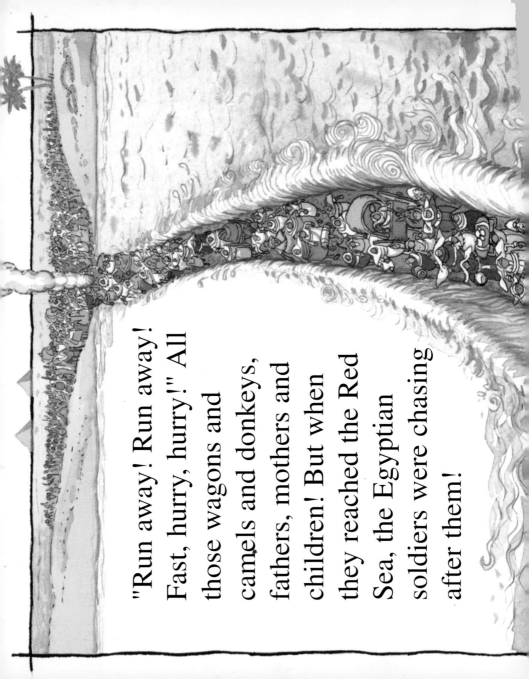

"Run away! Run away! Fast, hurry, hurry!" All those wagons and camels and donkeys, fathers, mothers and children! But when they reached the Red Sea, the Egyptian soldiers were chasing after them!

Take a bowl of water and blow as hard as you can to make the water split in two.

And the Egyptian soldiers? What happened to them when they started after the Hebrews? As soon as they reached the middle of the sea, crash! The waves drowned them all.

God wanted to take his people out of Egypt and bring them through the desert to a new homeland. But first they had to learn to trust God every day for food and water.

Go get a piece of bread from the kitchen. Mmmm, that smells good, doesn't it? That's what the children in the desert said when God sent little flakes of bread falling from the sky.

God's people grumbled because they didn't trust Moses. And they didn't trust God. This was wrong. Only when we trust, can God take care of us.

Are you hungry now? Listen to your stomach when you're hungry. It grumbles. That's what God's people did in the desert. They grumbled a lot.

God gave Moses ten rules to follow, written in stone, so God's people could be safe and healthy.

Go find a rock and try to write on it with YOUR finger.

34

When Moses was on the mountain, God came down from his cloud to be with Moses. Moses shut his eyes tight, God's glory was so great.

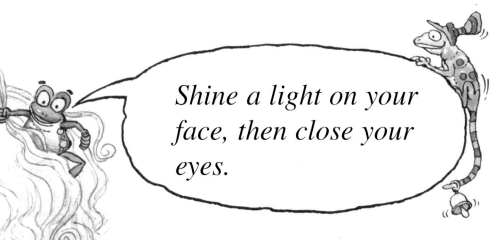

Shine a light on your face, then close your eyes.

It took God's people forty years to reach God's promised land called Canaan. All that time God had taken good care of His people, giving them food and water every day.

A NOTE TO THE big PEOPLE:

The *Little Children's Bible Books* may be your child's first introduction to the Bible, God's Word. This story of *Moses* is based on the book of Exodus, and the book of Numbers, chapters 9-14. It makes these parts of the Bible spring to life. This is a DO book. Point things out, ask your child to find, seek, say, and discover.

Before you read these stories, pray that your child's little heart would be touched by the love of God. These stories are about planting seeds, having vision, learning right from wrong, and choosing to believe. *Moses* is one of the first steps on the way. The Bible story is told in straight type.

A LITTLE something fun is written in italics by the narrating animal . . .

. . . to make the story come alive. In this DO book, wave, wink, hop, roar or do any of the other things the stories suggest so this can become a fun time of growing closer.

Pray together after you read this . . . together. There's no better way for big people to learn from little people.